Fit and Fun

BY MEGAN BAILEY

The Child's World

Published by The Child's World®
1980 Lookout Drive • Mankato, MN 56003-1705
800-599-READ • www.childsworld.com

Acknowledgments
The Child's World®: Mary Berendes, Publishing Director
Red Line Editorial: Editorial direction
The Design Lab: Design
Amnet: Production
Photographs ©: Front cover: PhotoDisc; Kids in Motion; PhotoDisc, 3,
21 (top-left), 21 (top-right), 23; Kids in Motion, 4, 10, 11, 12, 18, 19, 21
(bottom-left), 21 (bottom-right), 21 (top-middle); BrandX Images, 5, 6, 9,
17; Comstock, 7, 14, 16; Rob Marmion/Shutterstock, 11; FoodIcons, 13

ISBN: 978-1623235437
LCCN: 2013931364

Printed in the United States of America
Mankato, MN
July, 2013
PA02174

ABOUT THE AUTHOR

Megan Bailey is a freelance writer who
works from her home in Chicago. She loves
kids and pets, especially cats, and the
Chicago Cubs.

Table of Contents

CHAPTER ONE

Fitness Is Fun!

It is Molly's first day of third grade at her new school. She is worried about making friends. Will the kids at this new school be nice?

That morning, Molly's teacher walks the class over for gym class. As they enter the gym, Mrs. Tyler, the gym teacher, passes out slips of paper to each student. Mrs. Tyler explains that on each slip is the name of a classmate. This classmate is

◄ *Have fun and stay healthy with a fitness buddy.*

▶ *Gym class games such as tug-of-war are great ways to stay active.*

▲ *Fun physical activities can help you stay fit and healthy.*

◄ *Opposite page: Get friends together for a basketball game.*

to be their fitness buddy for the week. She says that their homework assignment is to spend some time with their buddy doing a fun fitness activity, such as playing tag or going for a bike ride. Mrs. Tyler challenges them to do a **physical** activity together for an hour each day. Being physically active for an hour every day is one of the best ways to stay physically fit.

That day after school, Molly meets her fitness buddy, Jessica, at the park for the first day of their assignment. Molly is happy that Jessica is so friendly and is excited about Mrs. Tyler's challenge. Jessica suggests spending their fitness time seeing who can swing the highest on the swings and who can climb across the monkey bars the fastest.

Each day their fitness buddy time is more fun than the last! They play hide-and-seek, they go on a bike ride, and they even do some skateboarding. By the end of the week, Molly and Jessica are great friends. They both learned that fitness is an important way to stay healthy and that fitness can be a lot of fun.

Physical fitness is staying active to keep your body and mind healthy. Physical fitness helps you build strong muscles and bones and can even help your body fight illness.

There are many different ways you can stay active. A popular type of physical fitness is **aerobic activity**. Aerobic activity is when you move your body to make your heart pump your blood faster and to make your lungs work harder. It can also make your body produce sweat. Aerobic activity can be a lot of fun! Skateboarding, swimming, riding your bike,

Doctors recommend that children and teenagers get at least 60 minutes of physical activity a day, five days a week. Adults should aim for 30 minutes of physical activity, five days a week. This might sound like a lot of time, but time spent being physically active can add up quickly in one day! Think about how long it would take you to walk or ride your bike to school and back.

▶ *Opposite page: Riding your bike is an aerobic activity.*

and dancing are just a few examples of aerobic activity.

Physical fitness also includes activities other than aerobic ones. Activities that stretch your muscles and keep them strong are important, too. These activities are called **anaerobic activities** and include push-ups, sit-ups, and **yoga**. Yoga is an exercise system that began in India about 5,000 years ago. In yoga, people hold different poses that help them

◄ *Stretching and yoga are activities that can help you relax.*

stretch their muscles and concentrate on their breathing. Many people find that stretching and breathing help them relax.

▶ *Yoga is an anaerobic activity.*

CHAPTER TWO

Keeping Your Body and Mind Healthy

Being physically fit has many benefits. It is an excellent way to keep your body healthy and feeling good. When you do a physical activity, such as jumping rope, your heart begins to pump your blood faster and your lungs begin to work harder, too. This makes your heart and lungs even stronger. Physical activity can make your muscles and bones stronger as well.

Physical fitness also helps your body stay at a healthy weight. Physical activity helps your body

▲ *Jump rope to get your blood pumping.*

burn off **calories**. A calorie is a measurement of energy that your body gets from food.

▶ *Healthy snacks like cherries are good fuel for physical activities.*

Without calories, our bodies would not have enough energy for physical activities. But if your body has too many calories, it can cause you to gain weight. Gaining too much weight can cause **obesity**. Obesity is when a person weighs much more than what is healthy for his or her body.

Physical activity also is good for your mind. When you **participate** in a physical activity, your body releases **endorphins**. Endorphins are chemicals your body creates that can make you feel happy and relaxed. Staying physically fit may also improve your **self-esteem**. Developing your skills in team sports and other activities can help you feel respect for yourself and your abilities.

CALORIES COUNT!
The average kid needs to eat about 1,600–2,500 calories a day. Counting calories is not recommended for most kids. Typically, kids can count on their bodies to let them know when they need to eat. If you feel you may be overweight and are thinking about going on a diet, you should speak to a doctor for advice first. Talking to a doctor about these decisions is important to make sure you stay healthy.

▶ *Opposite page: Playing team sports can help build your self-esteem.*

CHAPTER THREE

Fun with Fitness!

Physical fitness activities can be a lot of fun whether you do them by yourself or with other people. Playing a team sport, such as basketball or baseball, is a great way to have fun and stay physically fit. Team sports can teach you how to work well with other people. When participating in team sports, you learn how to have good **sportsmanship**. Good sportsmanship means playing by the rules of the game and showing respect to the people on your team and the team you are playing against.

▼ *Participate in a team sport like baseball to learn good sportsmanship and stay active.*

Physical fitness can also be a great way to spend time with your family and friends. Activities such as going to the park, walking the dog, or playing catch are some fun things to do with other people. Try making a fitness plan with your family by taking turns picking a physical activity to do together. You never know, Mom and Dad just

► *Riding bikes with friends can be a fun activity.*

might teach you a new,
fun activity!

Sometimes your friends
and parents might be too busy
to participate in a physical
activity, but that does not
mean you have to sit in
front of the TV. There
are plenty of physical
activities that are fun to

◄ *If you cannot find a fitness buddy,
take your pet for a walk or run.*

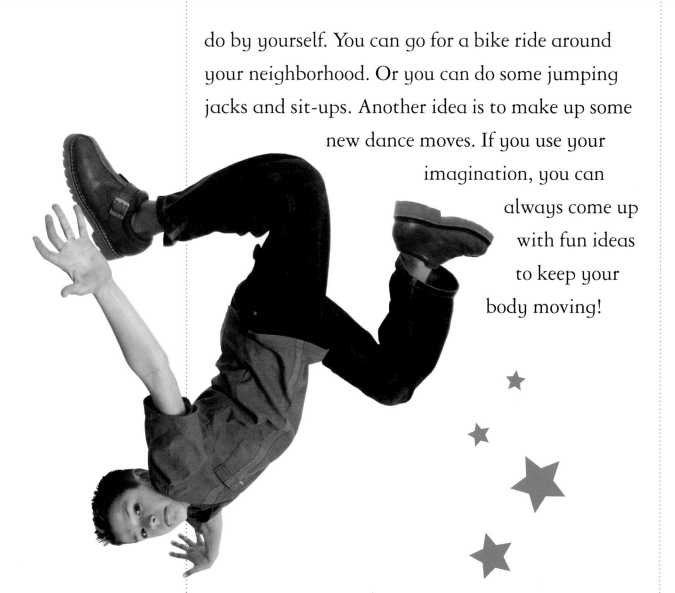

do by yourself. You can go for a bike ride around your neighborhood. Or you can do some jumping jacks and sit-ups. Another idea is to make up some new dance moves. If you use your imagination, you can always come up with fun ideas to keep your body moving!

Hands-on Activity: Fit and Fun Collage

A Fit and Fun Collage is a way to get creative and come up with different ideas about physical fitness.

What You'll Need:

Poster board, glue, and magazines (or pictures on the computer)
Optional: Paint, markers, and glitter to decorate your collage

Directions:

1. First, go through magazines or find pictures on the computer of people participating in physical activities and print them out. Try to find pictures of some of the activities that are discussed in the book, such as yoga or team sports.
2. Next, cut out the pictures and glue them onto your poster board. Have fun with it! You can get creative and use paint, markers, and glitter to decorate your collage.
3. Finally, display your collage in a place where you can look at it every day as a way to inspire you to stay physically fit.

Glossary

aerobic activity (er-OH-bik ak-TIV-it-ee): Aerobic activity is moving your body to make your heart pump faster and to make your lungs work harder. Aerobic activity can also make your body produce sweat.

anaerobic activities (an-er-OH-bik ak-TIV-it-eez): Anaerobic activities are movements that help strengthen muscles by making them work hard in a short amount of time. Push-ups and sit-ups are examples of anaerobic activities.

calories (KAL-ur-eez): Calories are measurements of energy that your body gets from food. Eating too many calories may cause you to gain weight.

endorphins (en-DOR-fenz): Endorphins are chemicals your body releases that can make you feel happy and relaxed. Physical activity releases endorphins.

obesity (oh-BEES-it-ee): Obesity occurs when a person weighs much more than what is healthy for his or her body. Eating too many calories and not being physically active may lead to obesity.

participate (par-TIS-eh-payt): To participate is to take part in an activity. Some kids participate in team sports to stay active.

physical (FIZ-i-kul): Physical is a word used to describe things that relate to the body. For example, physical activity is activity that moves the body, making it stronger and healthier.

physical fitness (FIZ-i-kul FIT-nes): Physical fitness is being active to keep your body and mind healthy. Physical fitness helps you build strong muscles and bones and can even help your body fight illness.

self-esteem (self e-STEEM): Self-esteem is having respect for yourself and your skills. Physical fitness can improve your self-esteem.

sportsmanship (SPORTS-men-ship): Sportsmanship is playing by the rules of a game and showing respect to people on your team and the team you are playing against. Good sportsmanship is an important part of playing team sports.

yoga (YO-ga): Yoga is an exercise system that began in India about 5,000 years ago. In yoga, people hold different poses that help them stretch their muscles and focus on their breathing.

To Learn More

BOOKS

Kajander, Rebecca and Timothy Culbert. *Be Fit, Be Strong, Be You*. Minneapolis, MN: Free Spirit Publishing, Inc., 2010.

Smithyman, Kathryn and Bobbie Kalman. *Active Kids*. New York: Crabtree Publishing Company, 2003.

WEB SITES

Visit our Web site for links about physical fitness: **childsworld.com/links**

Note to Parents, Teachers, and Librarians: We routinely verify our Web links to make sure they are safe and active sites. So encourage your readers to check them out!

Index